MY WORLD in FRENCH

Coloring Book & Picture Dictionary

Tamara M. Mealer

PASSPORT BOOKS
a division of *NTC Publishing Group*

To the Parents and Teachers

Research has shown that the best way to help children learn a language is to involve them physically in the learning process. Entertaining, hands-on activities engage children's enthusiasm and encourage greater retention of learning.

My World in French has been created for today's young learner of French with these findings in mind. The coloring pages spark children's interest and involve them in hands-on activities. As they color, children will notice that some people or items in the pictures are numbered. They can look up the names of these people and items in French and English on the page opposite the picture. A pronunciation guide follows each French word to promote correct pronunciation. When the pictures have been colored, *My World in French* becomes a delightful picture dictionary that children have helped create themselves.

Each picture is also accompanied by a few questions designed to help children practice the words they are learning and encourage them to use the French names of items in the pictures. Use these questions as a guide for formulating more questions about the pictures and for starting conversations about the French words presented in each one. The more involved you become in a child's language-learning process, the more he or she will learn.

1993 Printing

Published by Passport Books, a division of NTC Publishing Group.
© 1992 by NTC Publishing Group, 4255 West Touhy Avenue,
Lincolnwood (Chicago), Illinois 60646-1975 U.S.A.
Manufactured in the United States of America.
2 3 4 5 6 7 8 9 ML 9 8 7 6 5 4 3

About This Book

This book will help you learn to talk about your world in French. You will find pictures of places you know, like the classroom, the kitchen, the beach, the zoo, the circus, and many more. Color the pictures any way you like!

While you are coloring, you will notice numbers next to some objects or people in the picture. Look at the same numbers on the page across from the picture. You will find the names of the people and objects next to the numbers. First, you will see the names in French. After each French word, you will see a pronunciation guide in parentheses. This tells you how to say the French word out loud. It may look funny, but if you read it out loud, you will be saying the word correctly. To find out more about how to say sounds in French and using the pronunciation guides, read the section called "How to Say French Sounds." Lastly, you will also find the name of each person or object in English.

The pages across from the pictures also have some questions about what you see in each picture. Try to answer the questions with the French words you have learned. The answers to the questions are in an answer key at the back of the book, but don't peek until you have tried to answer the questions yourself!

At the beginning of the book, there are some facts about the French language. Knowing these will help you when you use the words you have learned to talk about things in French.

Share this book with your parents or with your friends. Learning French is a lot of fun, but you will enjoy it even more if you do it with a friend. *Amuse-toi bien!* (IIave fun!)

Contents

Some Helpful Hints about French

Masculine and Feminine Words

In French, all nouns (people, places, and things) are either masculine or feminine. Words that have the word **la** before them are feminine. For example, **la maison** (house) is feminine. Words with **le** before them are masculine, so **le chien** (dog) is masculine. **Le** and **la** both mean "the" in French. They are usually used when you talk about people, places, and things. If a word begins with a vowel in French, then you will see **l'**, as in **l'arbre**. For these words, you must simply learn by heart whether they are masculine or feminine.

Talking about More than One

When you want to talk about more than one of something, just add the letter **s** to the end of a word. So when you want to talk about more than one **salon**, an **s** is added. More than one **fille** is **filles**. Remember that the **s** at the end of a word is not pronounced in French. Some words are different. For example, to talk about more than one **animal**, you say **animaux**. As you learn French, you will learn which words do not add **s** when you talk about more than one.

You must also change **le** and **la** when you talk about more than one of something. **Le** and **la** become **les**. For example, to talk about more than one mirror, you say **les miroirs**. To talk about more than one animal, you say **les animaux**.

How to Say French Sounds

In French, many letters are said in a different way from English. The best way to learn to say French sounds is to listen to French-speaking people and copy what they say. But here are some rules to help you.

Below is a list of letters, with a guide to show you how to say each one. For each French sound, there is an English word (or part of a word) that sounds like it. Read it out loud to find out how to say the French sound. Then, practice saying the examples for each sound.

a	Often like the "a" sound in "cart": **acrob<u>a</u>te, ch<u>a</u>t, h<u>a</u>rpe, gir<u>a</u>fe.**
e	Like the "a" sound in "above": **l<u>e</u>, quatr<u>e</u>, sab<u>le</u>.**
e at the end of words	An "e" at the end of a word is usually silent: **adress<u>e</u>, antenn<u>e</u>, glac<u>e</u>.** Except for words that end in a consonant + *re* or a consonant + *le*. Then, the "e" has the "a" sound in "above": **quatr<u>e</u>, sab<u>le</u>, jong<u>le</u>.**
é	Like the "ay" sound in "late": **<u>é</u>l<u>é</u>phant, d<u>é</u>fil<u>é</u>, r<u>é</u>frig<u>é</u>rateur.**
è	Like the "a" sound in "care": **p<u>è</u>re, cr<u>è</u>me, sali<u>è</u>re.**
ê	Like the "e" sound in "get": **for<u>ê</u>t, arr<u>ê</u>t, fen<u>ê</u>tre.**
i, y	Like the "i" in "machine": **g<u>i</u>let, lund<u>i</u>, h<u>y</u>draulique.**
o	Like the "o" in "go": **cap<u>o</u>t, fr<u>o</u>mage, v<u>o</u>lant.**
u	To say this sound, hold your mouth as if to make the "ee" sound and shape your lips as if to make the "oo" sound: **men<u>u</u>, pl<u>u</u>me, spat<u>u</u>le.**
eau, au	Like the "oa" sound in "toast": **dinos<u>au</u>re, <u>au</u>bergine, <u>eau</u>, tabl<u>eau</u>.**
eu	Like the "u" sound in "fur": **f<u>eu</u>, j<u>eu</u>, tract<u>eu</u>r.**
ou	Like the "oo" sound in "food": **l<u>ou</u>che, m<u>ou</u>ton, p<u>ou</u>belle.**

oi	Like the "wo" sound in "wobble": t**oi**t, p**oi**re, framb**oi**se.
on, an, en	Like "ong" without the "g" sound at the end: avi**on**, gr**an**ge, li**on**, m**an**che.
in, ain, im	Like the "an" sound in "rang" without the "g" at the end: b**ain**, **in**strument, **im**perméable.
c	Before "i" or "e," it sounds like the "s" in "sun": **c**irque, ordonnan**c**e, gla**c**e. Before other letters, it sounds like the "c" in "cat": a**c**robate, **c**rabe, fa**c**teur.
ch	Like the "sh" sound in "shirt": **ch**at, **ch**èvre, lou**ch**e.
g	Before "i" or "e," it sounds like the "s" sound in "measure": **g**irafe, oran**g**e, nei**g**e. Before other letters, it is like the "g" in "get": **g**lobe, **g**omme, rè**g**le.
j	Like the "s" sound in "measure": **j**ambon, **j**ournal, **j**udo.
qu	Like the "k" sound in "kite": **qu**atre, pi**qu**e-ni**qu**e, bouti**qu**e.
r	Make this sound at the back of your throat, a little like gargling: ma**r**di, **r**ame, t**r**ain.
h	This letter is silent: **h**arpe, **h**erbe, **h**ache.
w	Like the "v" sound in "vacation": **w**agon.

A consonant at the end of a French word is usually silent: vagabon**d**, cha**t**, cano**t**.

After each French word in this book, you will find a pronunciation guide in parentheses. This is a special spelling that tells you how to say the word correctly. It may look funny, but if you read the pronunciation guide out loud, you will be saying the word correctly.

In the pronunciation guides, we've given special spellings for sounds that are not found in English. The "eu" sound is spelled **ER**, the "ain, in, im" sound is spelled **IN**, and the "an, on, en" sound is spelled **ON**. The "oi" sound is spelled **wa,** and whenever a pair of letters sounds like the "igh" in "night," it is spelled **igh.** The sound of the letter "e" in French is spelled **uh.**

One last hint: when you see the letter "e" in the pronunciation guides, say it like the "e" in "get," even when it comes before the letter "r."

You should also remember that every word also has a stressed syllable. This is the syllable that must be said a little louder than the others. In French, the last syllable is always stressed, so always say the last syllable of a word a little louder than the others.

More Useful Words in French

Here are a few useful words that are not included in the pictures:

Les jours de la semaine

lundi	Monday
mardi	Tuesday
mercredi	Wednesday
jeudi	Thursday
vendredi	Friday
samedi	Saturday
dimanche	Sunday

Days of the Week

Les mois de l'année

janvier	January
février	February
mars	March
avril	April
mai	May
juin	June
juillet	July
août	August
septembre	September
octobre	October
novembre	November
décembre	December

Months of the Year

1. Notre maison (no-truh may-zON)   Our House

1. **les montagnes** (lay mON-tan-yuh)   mountains
2. **les arbres** (layz ar-bruh)   trees
3. **la muraille en briques** (la mu-righ ON breek)   brick fence
4. **le pin** (luh pIN)   pine tree
5. **le garage** (luh ga-raj)   garage
6. **la pierre** (la pyayr)   stone
7. **la piscine** (la pee-seen)   swimming pool
8. **la fourche à bêcher** (la foorsh a be-shay)   gardening fork
9. **la pelle** (la pel)   gardening shovel
10. **le trou** (luh troo)   hole
11. **la terre** (la ter)   soil
12. **la boîte aux lettres** (la bwat o let-ruh)   mailbox
13. **la brouette** (la broo-et)   wheelbarrow

14. **les fleurs** (lay flERr)   flowers
15. **la branche d'arbre** (la brONsh dar-bruh)   tree branch
16. **les feuilles** (lay fERy)   leaves
17. **le chenil** (luh shuh-neel)   doghouse
18. **le chien** (luh shyIN)   dog
19. **le jardinier** (luh jar-dee-nyay)   gardener
20. **le râteau** (luh ra-to)   rake
21. **le tuyau d'arrosage** (luh tuee-yo da-ro-zaj)   watering hose
22. **le jet** (luh jay)   nozzle
23. **les meubles de patio** (lay mER-bluh duh pa-tyo)   patio furniture
24. **les arbustes** (layz ar-bust)   bushes
25. **les lumières externes** (lay lu-myayr ex-tern)   outdoor lights
26. **la cheminée** (la shuh-mee-nay)   chimney
27. **le toit** (luh twa)   roof
28. **l'échandole** (lay-shON-dol)   shingle
29. **la gouttière** (la goo-tyayr)   gutter
30. **le vitre** (luh vee-truh)   glass
31. **la clôture en lattes** (la klo-tur ON lat)   wooden fence

Questions

1. What is "le tuyau d'arrosage"?
2. What tools is the woman using?
3. Name the two types of fences.
4. Who is raking the leaves?

2. Le salon (luh sa-lON)   The Living Room

1. **l'antenne** (lON-ten)   antenna
2. **la radio** (la ra-dyo)   radio
3. **le tourne-disques** (luh toor-nuh-deesk)   record player
4. **la machine à écrire** (la ma-sheen a ay-kreer)   typewriter
5. **les disques** (lay deesk)   records
6. **la télévision** (la tay-lay-vee-zyON)   television
7. **la bibliothèque** (la bee-blee-o-tek)   bookcase
8. **le livre** (luh lee-vruh)   book
9. **le tapis** (luh ta-pee)   carpet
10. **le téléphone** (luh tay-lay-fon)   telephone
11. **le canapé** (luh ka-na-pay)   sofa
12. **les aiguilles à tricoter** (layz ay-guee a tree-ko-tay)   knitting needles
13. **le fil de laine** (luh feel duh len)   yarn
14. **la table de salon** (la ta-bluh duh sa-lON)   coffee table
15. **l'enveloppe** (lON-vlop)   envelope
16. **la lettre** (la let-ruh)   letter
17. **le journal** (luh joor-nal)   newspaper
18. **la grand-mère** (la grON-mayr)   grandmother
19. **l'oreiller** (lo-ray-yay)   pillow
20. **l'aspirateur** (las-pee-ra-tERr)   vacuum cleaner
21. **le fauteuil à bascule** (luh fo-tERy a bas-kul)   rocking chair
22. **le petit-fils** (luh puh-tee fees)   grandson
23. **le chat** (luh sha)   cat

24. **le panier à bois** (luh pa-nyay a bwa)   log basket
25. **les bûches** (lay bush)   logs
26. **le carrelage** (luh kar-laj)   floor tile
27. **le feu** (luh fER)   fire
28. **le manteau de cheminée** (luh mON-to duh shuh-mee-nay)   mantel
29. **la pendule** (la pON-dul)   clock
30. **la console murale** (la kON-sol mu-ral)   wall bracket
31. **l'abat-jour** (la-ba-joor)   lamp shade
32. **le miroir** (luh meer-war)   mirror
33. **le cadre** (luh ka-druh)   frame
34. **les rideaux** (lay ree-do)   curtains
35. **le parapluie** (luh pa-ra-pluee)   umbrella
36. **le porte-parapluies** (luh port pa-ra-pluee)   umbrella stand
37. **le fauteuil** (luh fo-tERy)   armchair
38. **la plante** (la plONt)   plant
39. **la photo** (la fo-to)   photograph

Questions

1. What does the grandmother have in her hands?
2. Who is playing with "le chat"?
3. What is on the mantel?
4. What is the boy near the shelves looking for?

3. La cuisine (la kuee-zeen)   The Kitchen

1. **le détergent à vaisselle** (luh day-tayr-jON a vay-sel)   dish detergent
2. **la brosse de cuisine** (la bros duh kuee-zeen)   dish brush
3. **le placard de cuisine** (luh pla-kar duh kuee-zeen)   kitchen cabinet
4. **le livre de cuisine** (luh lee-vruh duh kuee-zeen)   cookbook
5. **l'évier** (lay-vyay)   sink
6. **le robinet** (luh ro-bee-nay)   faucet
7. **la manche** (la mONsh)   handle
8. **le hachoir** (luh ash-war)   chopping block
9. **la machine à laver la vaisselle** (la ma-sheen a la-vay la vay-sel)   dishwasher
10. **le tiroir** (luh teer-war)   drawer
11. **l'atomiseur** (la-to-mee-zERr)   sprayer
12. **la poudre à nettoyer** (la poo-druh a net-twa-yay)   cleanser
13. **les verres** (lay ver)   glasses
14. **le rouleau à pâtisserie** (luh roo-lo a pa-tees-ree)   rolling pin
15. **le jambon en boîte** (luh jON-bON ON bwat)   canned ham
16. **le tamis** (luh ta-mee)   sifter
17. **le grille-pain** (luh gree-pIN)   toaster
18. **le pain grillé** (luh pIN gree-yay)   toast
19. **la spatule** (la spa-tul)   spatula
20. **la confiture** (la kON-fee-tur)   jam
21. **le mixer** (luh meek-sERr)   blender
22. **le verre gradué** (luh ver-gra-duay)   measuring cup
23. **le bol** (luh bol)   bowl
24. **le batteur** (luh ba-tERr)   hand mixer
25. **la salière** (la sa-lyayr)   salt shaker
26. **la poivrière** (la pwav-ryayr)   pepper shaker
27. **la louche** (la loosh)   ladle
28. **le presse-purée** (luh pres-pu-ray)   potato masher
29. **les cuillères à mesurer** (lay kuee-yayr a muh-zu-ray)   measuring spoons
30. **les serviettes en papier** (lay ser-vyet ON pa-pyay)   paper napkins
31. **la fourchette** (la foor-shet)   fork
32. **le couteau** (luh koo-to)   knife
33. **les cuillères** (lay kuee-yayr)   spoons
34. **le beurre** (luh bERr)   butter

35. **le chien** (luh shyIN)   dog
36. **l'eau** (lo)   water
37. **le café** (luh ka-fay)   coffee
38. **le couvercle** (luh koo-ver-kluh)   lid
39. **la serpillière** (la ser-pee-yayr)   mop
40. **le seau** (luh so)   bucket
41. **le chiffon** (luh shee-fON)   rag
42. **le rôti de bœuf** (luh ro-tee duh bERf)   roast beef
43. **le four** (luh foor)   oven
44. **la casserole** (la kas-rol)   pan
45. **la bouilloire** (la booy-war)   tea kettle
46. **la cuisinière** (la kuee-zee-nyayr)   range
47. **les œufs** (layz ER)   eggs
48. **la poêle** (la pwal)   frying pan
49. **la mère** (la mer)   mother
50. **la pelle à poussière** (la pel a poo-syer)   dustpan
51. **la poubelle** (la poo-bel)   trash can
52. **le réfrigérateur** (luh ray-free-jay-ra-tERr)   refrigerator
53. **la lampe de poche** (la lONp duh posh)   flashlight
54. **le congélateur** (luh kON-jay-la-tERr)   freezer
55. **le torchon** (luh tor-shON)   dish cloth
56. **la lessive** (la le-seev)   laundry detergent
57. **la machine à laver** (la ma-sheen a la-vay)   washer
58. **le séchoir** (luh sesh-war)   dryer
59. **le balai** (luh ba-lay)   broom
60. **le porte-lettres** (luh por-tuh-let-ruh)   letter holder
61. **le panier à pique-nique** (luh pa-nyay a peek-neek)   picnic basket
62. **le seau à glace** (luh so a glas)   ice bucket
63. **les tasses** (lay tas)   cups

Questions

1. What is in "le four"?
2. What is "le chien" drinking?
3. What is in the toaster?
4. What is in the bucket?

4. En classe (ON klas)   In the Classroom

1. **le dinosaure** (luh dee-no-zor)   dinosaur
2. **l'horloge** (lor-loj)   clock
3. **le plafond** (luh-pla-fON)   ceiling
4. **l'alphabet** (lal-fa-bay)   alphabet
5. **le bureau** (luh bu-ro)   desk
6. **le vase** (luh vaz)   vase
7. **le lapin** (luh la-pIN)   rabbit
8. **le tableau noir** (luh ta-blo nwar)   blackboard
9. **la soustraction** (la soo-strak-syON)   subtraction
10. **la multiplication** (la mul-tee-plee-ka-syON)   multiplication
11. **l'addition** (la-dee-syON)   addition
12. **le placard** (luh pla-kar)   closet
13. **le calendrier** (luh ka-lON-dree-yay)   calendar
14. **la photo** (la fo-to)   photograph
15. **les billes** (lay beey)   marbles
16. **le globe** (luh glob)   globe
17. **les livres** (lay lee-vruh)   books
18. **les poupées** (lay poo-pay)   dolls
19. **les boîtes** (lay bwat)   boxes
20. **la colle** (la kol)   glue
21. **la marionnette en papier** (la ma-ryo-net ON pa-pyay)   paper puppet
22. **le sac en papier** (luh sak ON pa-pyay)   paper bag
23. **le ruban adhésif** (luh ru-bON a-day-zeef)   adhesive tape
24. **les ciseaux** (lay see-zo)   scissors
25. **l'argile** (lar-jeel)   clay
26. **la cage** (la kaj)   cage

ABCDEFGHIJKLMNOPQRSTU

27. **les crayons de couleur** (lay kray-ON duh koo-lERr) crayons
28. **la règle** (la re-gluh) ruler
29. **le pinceau** (luh pIN-so) paintbrush
30. **la craie** (la kray) chalk
31. **la peinture** (la pIN-tur) paint
32. **les punaises** (lay pu-nez) tacks
33. **le jeu de construction** (luh jER duh kON-struk-syON) building blocks
34. **le chevalet** (luh shuh-va-lay) easel
35. **l'aquarelle** (la-kwa-rel) watercolor
36. **la blouse** (la blooz) smock
37. **la gomme** (la gom) eraser
38. **le papier** (luh pa-pyay) paper
39. **les crayons** (lay kray-ON) pencils
40. **l'étudiant** (lay-tu-dyON) student
41. **la poubelle** (la poo-bel) wastebasket
42. **les dessins** (lay des-sIN) drawings
43. **l'aquarium** (la-kwa-ryuhm) aquarium
44. **les poissons** (lay pwa-sON) fish
45. **la fenêtre** (la fuh-ne-truh) window
46. **le cochon** (luh ko-shON) pig
47. **l'oiseau** (lwa-zo) bird
48. **le chat** (luh sha) cat
49. **le singe** (luh sINj) monkey
50. **la carte** (la kart) map
51. **le taille-crayon** (luh tigh-kray-ON) pencil sharpener
52. **le plumier** (luh plu-myay) pencil holder
53. **le cahier** (luh ka-yay) notebook
54. **l'institutrice** (lIN-stee-tu-trees) teacher

Questions

1. What do you use to cut paper?
2. Name the three math problems on the blackboard.
3. What is the girl at the easel wearing?
4. Name the objects hanging on the left wall.

5. Les vêtements (lay vet-mON) Clothing

1. **le chapeau** (luh sha-po) hat
2. **les lunettes** (lay lu-net) glasses
3. **la robe** (la rob) dress
4. **le maillot de bain** (luh migh-yo duh bIN) bathing suit
5. **le sac** (luh sak) purse
6. **les bottes de neige** (lay bot duh nej) snow boots
7. **les pantoufles** (lay pON-toof-luh) slippers
8. **les chaussures à talons hauts** (lay sho-sur a ta-lON o) high-heeled shoes
9. **le pull** (luh pul) sweater
10. **la jupe** (la jup) skirt
11. **les chaussures** (lay sho-sur) shoes
12. **les sandales** (lay sON-dal) sandals

13. **la veste** (la vest)   jacket
14. **la casquette** (la kas-ket)   cap
15. **le manteau** (luh mON-to)   coat
16. **la cravate** (la kra-vat)   tie
17. **le nœud papillon** (luh nER pa-pee-yON)   bow tie
18. **l'imperméable** (lIN-per-may-ab-luh)   rain coat
19. **la chemise à manches longues** (la shuh-meez a mONsh lONg)
    long-sleeved shirt
20. **le gilet** (luh jee-lay)   vest
21. **la ceinture** (la sIN-tur)   belt
22. **le peignoir** (luh payn-war)   bathrobe
23. **le pantalon** (luh pON-ta-lON)   pants
24. **le slip** (luh sleep)   underpants
25. **les chaussettes** (lay sho-set)   socks
26. **le pyjama** (luh pee-ja-ma)   pajamas
27. **les chaussures de tennis** (lay sho-sur duh tay-nees)   tennis shoes

Questions

1. What do you wear to help you see better?
2. What do you wear to bed?
3. What do you wear inside your shoes?
4. What do you wear to go swimming?

6. Les saisons et le temps (lay say-zON ay luh tON)

The Seasons and the Weather

1. **l'été** (lay-tay)   summer
2. **le printemps** (luh prIN-tON)   spring
3. **l'hiver** (lee-ver)   winter
4. **l'automne** (lo-ton)   fall

5. **le soleil** (luh so-lay)   sun
6. **les nuages** (lay nu-aj)   clouds
7. **la lune** (la lun)   moon
8. **l'arc-en-ciel** (lark-ON-syel)   rainbow
9. **chaud** (sho)   hot
10. **l'éclair** (lay-kler)   lightning
11. **la pluie** (la pluee)   rain
12. **froid** (frwa)   cold
13. **la neige** (la nej)   snow

Questions

1. What do you see after it rains?
2. What is the warmest season of the year?
3. What do you see during a thunderstorm?
4. What do you see in the sky at night?

7. Les sports (lay spor)   Sports

1. **l'escrime** (les-kreem)   fencing
2. **le tennis** (luh tay-nees)   tennis
3. **la lutte** (la lut)   wrestling
4. **le cyclisme** (luh seek-leesm)   cycling
5. **le ski** (luh skee)   skiing
6. **le bowling** (luh bo-ling)   bowling
7. **le basket-ball** (luh bas-ket-bal)   basketball

8. **la boxe** (la box)   boxing
9. **le base-ball** (luh bays-bal)   baseball
10. **le judo** (luh ju-do)   judo
11. **le ski nautique** (luh skee no-teek)   waterskiing
12. **le football américain** (luh foot-bal a-may-ree-kIN)   football

Questions

1. For which sport do you need a bat?
2. For which sports do you need skis?
3. Name a sport for which you need a bicycle.
4. What sport do you play in a bowling alley?

8. La ville (la veel)   The City

1. l'immeuble (lee-mER-bluh)   building
2. la boutique de fleuriste (la boo-teek duh flER-reest)   flower shop
3. le magasin de jouets (luh ma-ga-zIN duh joo-ay)   toy store
4. l'arrêt d'autobus (la-ray do-to-bus)   bus stop
5. le banc (luh bON)   bench
6. la boulangerie (la boo-lONj-ree)   bakery
7. la banne (la ban)   awning
8. le piéton (luh pyay-tON)   pedestrian
9. l'autobus scolaire (lo-to-bus sko-layr)   school bus
10. le conducteur (luh kON-duk-tERr)   driver
11. la camionnette (la ka-myo-net)   van
12. le feu rouge (luh fER rooj)   traffic lights
13. le taxi (luh ta-ksee)   taxi
14. la rue (la ru)   street
15. le camion (luh ka-myON)   truck
16. la station-service (la sta-syON-ser-vees)   gas station
17. la pompe à essence (la pONp a ay-sONs)   gas pump

18. **le passage clouté** (luh pa-saj kloo-tay)   pedestrian crossing
19. **le bulldozer** (luh bul-do-zer)   bulldozer
20. **le tuyau** (luh tuee-yo)   pipe
21. **le trou** (luh troo)   hole
22. **la boîte aux lettres** (la bwat o let-ruh)   mailbox
23. **le réverbère** (luh ray-ver-ber)   street light
24. **le pompier** (luh pON-pyay)   fireman
25. **la hache** (la ash)   axe
26. **l'échelle** (lay-shel)   ladder
27. **la voiture de pompiers** (la vwa-tur duh pON-pyay)   fire truck
28. **le gendarme** (luh jON-darm)   policeman
29. **l'accident** (lak-see-dON)   collision
30. **la sirène** (la see-ren)   siren
31. **la voiture de police** (la vwa-tur duh po-lees)   police car
32. **la bouche d'incendie** (la boosh dIN-sON-dee)   fire hydrant
33. **l'arbre** (lar-bruh)   tree
34. **l'ambulance** (lON-bu-lONs)   ambulance
35. **la dépanneuse** (la day-pa-nERz)   tow truck
36. **le parcmètre** (luh park-met-ruh)   parking meter
37. **la cour de récréation** (la koor duh ray-kray-a-syON)   playground

Questions

1. What happened to the two cars in the intersection?
2. If you are hurt, you are taken to the hospital in _____.
3. Who is directing the traffic?
4. What is "le pompier"?

9. Au supermarché (o su-per-mar-shay)   At the Supermarket

1. la glace (la glas)   ice cream
2. la bouteille (la boo-tay)   bottle
3. le sucre (luh su-kruh)   sugar
4. le beurre de cacahouètes (luh bERr duh ka-ka-wet)   peanut butter
5. la glace au chocolat (la glas o sho-ko-la)   chocolate ice cream
6. la boîte de conserve (la bwat de kON-serv)   can
7. le chariot (luh sha-ryo)   shopping cart
8. la confiture (la kON-fee-tur)   jam
9. le pain (luh pIN)   bread
10. la balance (la ba-lONs)   scale
11. les cerises (lay sER-reez)   cherries
12. les framboises (lay frON-bwaz)   raspberries
13. le raisin (luh ray-zIN)   grapes
14. les bananes (lay ba-nan)   bananas
15. les papayes (lay pa-pigh)   papayas
16. les fraises (lay frez)   strawberries
17. les fruits (lay fruee)   fruit
18. l'épicier (lay-pee-syay)   grocer
19. les provisions (lay pro-vee-zyON)   groceries
20. le sac en papier (luh sak ON pa-pyay)   paper bag
21. la caissière (la kes-syer)   cashier
22. la caisse (la kes)   cash register
23. le reçu (luh rER-su)   receipt
24. le panier à provisions (luh pa-nyay a pro-vee-zyON)   grocery basket

PAIN

FRUITS

25. **les pommes de terre** (lay pom duh ter)   potatoes
26. **les carottes** (lay ka-rot)   carrots
27. **les oignons** (layz o-nyON)   onions
28. **les haricots** (lay a-ree-ko)   beans
29. **les tomates** (lay to-mat)   tomatoes
30. **les choux** (lay shoo)   cabbages
31. **les aubergines** (layz o-ber-jeen)   eggplants
32. **la laitue** (la lay-tu)   lettuce
33. **le maïs** (luh ma-ees)   corn
34. **les poires** (lay pwar)   pears
35. **les courges** (lay koorj)   squash
36. **les asperges** (layz as-perj)   asparagus
37. **les poivrons** (lay pwa-vrON)   bell peppers
38. **les choux-fleurs** (lay shoo-flERr)   cauliflower
39. **les prunes** (lay prun)   plums
40. **les citrons** (lay see-trON)   lemons
41. **les pêches** (lay pesh)   peaches
42. **les pommes** (lay pom)   apples
43. **le gâteau** (luh ga-to)   cake
44. **la tarte** (la tart)   pie
45. **la pâtisserie** (la pa-tee-sree)   cupcake
46. **le thon** (luh tON)   tuna
47. **le jus** (luh ju)   juice
48. **la crème** (la krem)   hand cream
49. **la farine** (la fa-reen)   flour
50. **les céréales** (lay say-ray-al)   cereal
51. **l'étagère** (lay-ta-jer)   shelf
52. **le travailleur** (luh tra-vigh-ERr)   worker
53. **les gâteaux secs** (lay ga-to sek)   cookies
54. **le lait** (luh lay)   milk
55. **le fromage** (luh fro-maj)   cheese
56. **les saucissons** (lay so-see-sON)   sausages
57. **les œufs** (layz ER)   eggs
58. **l'agneau** (la-nyo)   lamb
59. **le beurre** (luh bERr)   butter
60. **le poulet** (luh poo-lay)   chicken
61. **les crabes** (lay krab)   crabs
62. **le poisson** (luh pwa-sON)   fish

Questions

1. What is the girl getting from the freezer?
2. Name all the vegetables that start with the letter "c."
3. Who is behind the cash register?
4. Who is packing the groceries?

Desserts

Légumes

10. Au restaurant (o res-to-rON)   In the Restaurant

1. **la plante** (la plONt)   plant
2. **le pot à fleurs** (luh po a flERr)   flowerpot
3. **la cheminée** (la shuh-mee-nay)   fireplace
4. **la table** (la ta-bluh)   table
5. **la chaise** (la shez)   chair
6. **le verre** (luh ver)   glass
7. **l'assiette** (las-syet)   plate
8. **la nappe** (la nap)   tablecloth
9. **la salade** (la sa-lad)   salad
10. **les pinces** (lay pINs)   tongs
11. **la glace** (la glas)   ice
12. **le bifteck** (luh beef-tek)   steak
13. **le gâteau** (luh ga-to)   cake
14. **le bacon** (luh ba-kON)   bacon
15. **les œufs sur le plat** (layz ER sur luh pla)   fried eggs
16. **la théière** (lay tay-yer)   teapot
17. **le poulet rôti** (luh poo-lay ro-tee)   roast chicken
18. **le pichet** (luh pee-shay)   pitcher
19. **l'addition** (la-dee-syON)   check
20. **la confiture** (la kON-fee-tur)   jam
21. **le menu** (luh mER-nu)   menu
22. **le sel** (luh sel)   salt
23. **le poivre** (luh pwav-ruh)   pepper
24. **la soucoupe** (la soo-koop)   saucer
25. **la tasse** (la tas)   cup
26. **la serviette** (la ser-vyet)   napkin
27. **le sandwich** (luh sON-dweesh)   sandwich
28. **le hamburger** (luh ON-boor-gERr)   hamburger

29. **les saucisses** (lay so-sees)   sausages
30. **le salami** (luh sa-la-mee)   salami
31. **le chef** (luh shef)   chef
32. **la serveuse** (la ser-vERz)   waitress
33. **le tablier** (luh ta-blee-ay)   apron
34. **le bol en métal** (luh bol ON may-tal)   metal bowl
35. **le jambon** (luh jON-bON)   ham
36. **les œufs farcis** (layz ER far-see)   stuffed eggs
37. **le verre à pied** (luh ver a pyay)   goblet
38. **le thé** (luh tay)   tea
39. **la machine à trancher** (la ma-sheen a trON-shay)   meat slicer
40. **l'évier** (lay-vyay)   sink
41. **la vaisselle sale** (la vay-sel sal)   dirty dishes
42. **la cafetière** (la caf-tyer)   coffeepot

Questions

1. Who is cooking in the kitchen?
2. Who is bringing the salad bowl?
3. What is the boy eating?
4. What does the girl have in her hands?

11. La poste (la post)   The Post Office

1. **le drapeau** (luh dra-po)   flag
2. **la poste** (la post)   post office
3. **le dock** (luh dok)   loading dock
4. **l'entrée** (lON-tray)   entrance
5. **le camion postal** (luh ka-myON pos-tal)   mail truck
6. **la boîte aux lettres** (la bwat o let-ruh)   mailbox
7. **le facteur** (luh fak-tERr)   mail carrier
8. **le sac postal** (luh sak pos-tal)   mail bag
9. **le prix** (luh pree)   price
10. **la balance** (la ba-lONs)   scale
11. **le paquet** (luh pa-kay)   package
12. **le timbre** (luh tIN-bruh)   stamp
13. **la lettre** (la let-ruh)   letter
14. **l'adresse** (la-dres)   address
15. **l'employée des postes** (lON-plwa-yay day post)   postal worker
16. **la liasse de lettres** (la lyas duh let-ruh)   bundled letters
17. **le journal** (luh joor-nal)   newspaper
18. **les revues** (lay rER-vu)   magazines

Questions

1. Where do you go to mail letters?
2. What must you put on an envelope?
3. Who delivers the mail?
4. What is "le journal"?

12. La banque (la bONk) The Bank

1. le classeur (luh kla-sERr) file cabinet
2. le tableau (luh ta-blo) painting
3. le garde (luh gard) guard
4. le coffre-fort (luh kof-ruh-for) safe
5. le coffre (luh kof-ruh) safety deposit box
6. la cliente (la klee-ONt) client
7. le chéquier (luh she-kyay) checkbook
8. la carte de crédit (la kart duh kray-dee) credit card
9. les billets (lay bee-yay) bills
10. les pièces (lay pyes) coins
11. le bulletin de versement (luh bul-tIN duh ver-suh-mON) deposit slip
12. le stylo (luh stee-lo) pen
13. le chèque (luh shek) check
14. le sac à argent (luh sak a ar-jON) money bag
15. le caissier (luh kes-syay) bank teller

Questions

1. Name a place where you keep valuables.
2. Name a room where money is locked in.
3. Who is standing near the vault?
4. What do you need to make a deposit?

13. Chez le médecin (shay luh mayd-sIN)   The Doctor's Office

1. **la pression artérielle** (la pres-syON ar-tayr-yel)   blood pressure
2. **l'infirmière** (lIN-feer-myer)   nurse
3. **la montre** (la mON-truh)   watch
4. **le thermomètre** (luh ter-mo-met-ruh)   thermometer
5. **l'aiguille** (lay-gueey)   needle
6. **la seringue** (la suh-rINg)   syringe
7. **les médicaments** (lay may-dee-ka-mON)   pills
8. **le technicien** (luh tek-nee-syIN)   technician
9. **le gant** (luh gON)   glove
10. **le plâtre** (luh pla-truh)   cast
11. **le diagramme** (luh dya-gram)   eye chart
12. **l'examen de l'ouïe** (lex-a-mIN duh looee)   hearing test
13. **l'otoscope** (lo-to-skop)   otoscope
14. **le bébé** (luh bay-bay)   baby
15. **le stéthoscope** (luh stay-to-skop)   stethoscope
16. **le pédiatre** (luh pay-dee-a-truh)   pediatrician
17. **l'ordonnance** (lor-do-nONs)   prescription

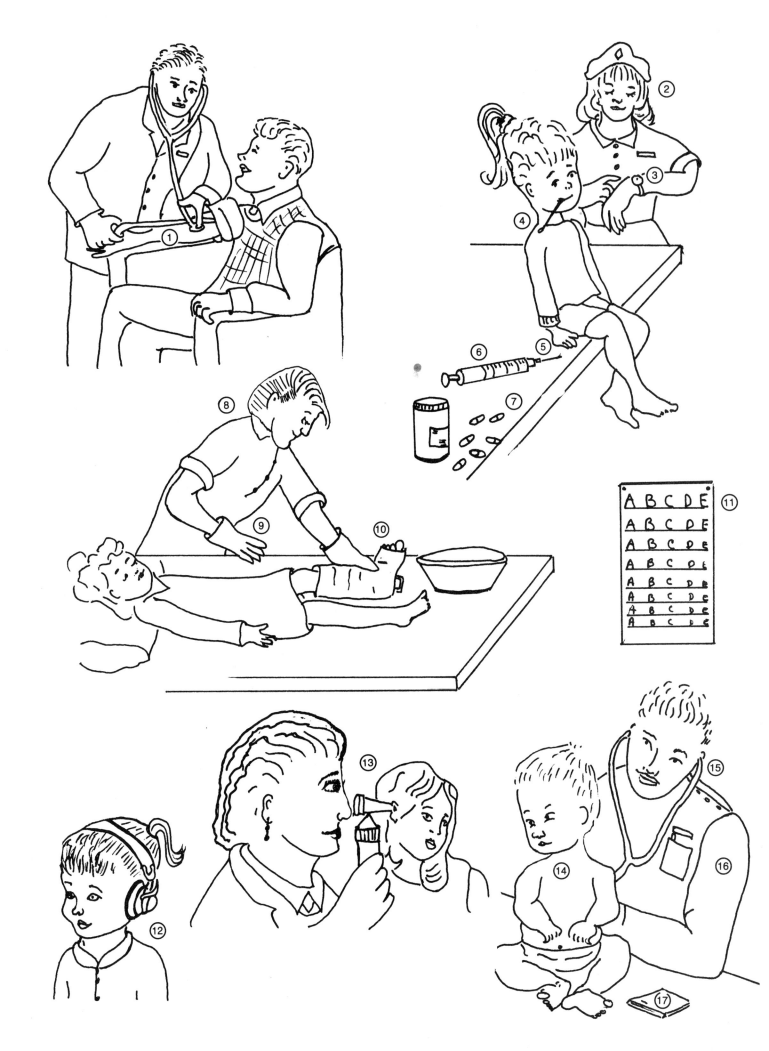

18. **le plombage** (luh plON-baj)   filling
19. **la fraise** (la frez)   drill
20. **la carie** (la ka-ree)   cavity
21. **les instruments dentaires** (layz IN-stru-mON dON-tayr)   dental instruments
22. **l'appareil dentaire** (la-pa-ray dON-tayr)   braces
23. **la radiographie** (la ra-dyo-gra-fee)   X ray
24. **l'orthopédiste** (lor-to-pay-deest)   orthopedist
25. **le pansement** (luh pONs-mON)   bandage
26. **le vétérinaire** (luh vay-tay-ree-nayr)   veterinarian
27. **l'ascenseur** (la-sON-sERr)   elevator
28. **la salle d'attente** (la sal da-tONt)   waiting room
29. **les béquilles** (lay bay-keey)   crutches
30. **le calendrier** (luh ka-lON-dryay)   calendar
31. **la réceptionniste** (la ray-sep-syo-neest)   receptionist
32. **le rendez-vous** (luh rON-day-voo)   appointment

Questions

1. What instrument is the doctor using to listen to the baby's heart?
2. What do you call an animal doctor?
3. Who is taking the girl's temperature?
4. What are "les béquilles"?

14. La station-service (la sta-syON-ser-vees)   The Service Station

1. l'ascenseur hydraulique (la-sON-sERr ee-dro-leek)   hydraulic lift
2. le pare-brise fêlé (luh par-breez fay-lay)   cracked windshield
3. le lave-auto (luh lav-o-to)   car wash
4. la portière cabossée (la por-tyer ka-bo-say)   dented door
5. la dépanneuse (la day-pa-nERz)   tow truck
6. la pompe à essence (la pomp a ay-sONs)   gas pump
7. l'employé (lON-plwa-yay)   attendant
8. le réservoir (luh ray-zer-vwar)   can
9. le bouchon de réservoir (luh boo-shON duh ray-zer-vwar)   gas cap
10. le coffre (luh kof-ruh)   trunk
11. le toit (luh twa)   roof
12. le siège (luh syej)   seat
13. la portière (la por-tyer)   door
14. le pneu (luh pnER)   tire
15. la plaque d'immatriculation (la plak dee-ma-tree-ku-la-syON)   license plate
16. le pare-chocs (luh par-shok)   bumper
17. le phare (luh far)   headlight
18. le capot (luh ka-po)   hood
19. l'essuie-glace (les-suee-glas)   windshield wiper
20. le volant (luh vo-lON)   steering wheel

21. **le bidon à huile** (luh bee-dON a ueel)   oil can
22. **le radiateur** (luh ra-dee-a-tERr)   radiator
23. **la boîte à outils** (la bwat a oo-tee)   toolbox
24. **la batterie** (la bat-ree)   battery
25. **les câbles volants** (lay ka-bluh vo-lON)   jumper cables
26. **le tournevis** (luh toor-nuh-vees)   screwdriver
27. **le marteau** (luh mar-to)   hammer
28. **la clef** (la klay)   wrench
29. **l'écrou** (lay-kroo)   nut
30. **la vis** (la vees)   screw
31. **la roue** (la roo)   wheel
32. **l'extincteur** (lex-tINk-tERr)   fire extinguisher
33. **les pneus** (lay pnER)   tires
34. **la pompe à air** (la pONp a ayr)   air pump
35. **le pneu crevé** (luh pnER crER-vay)   flat tire
36. **le mécanicien** (luh may-ka-nee-syIN)   mechanic

Questions

1. What do you call a person who repairs cars?
2. What is "le pare-chocs"?
3. What kind of truck do you see in this picture?
4. Name a place where you take the car to have it washed.

15. Le transport (luh trONs-por)   Transportation

1. **le monorail** (luh mo-no-righ)   monorail
2. **le train** (luh trIN)   train
3. **le funiculaire** (luh fu-nee-ku-layr)   cable car
4. **la voiture** (la vwa-tur)   automobile
5. **le camion** (luh ka-myON)   truck
6. **l'autobus** (lo-to-bus)   bus
7. **la moto** (la mo-to)   motorcycle
8. **le vélo** (luh vay-lo)   bicycle

9. **l'avion** (la-vyON)   airplane
10. **la montgolfière** (la mON-gol-fyer)   hot-air balloon
11. **le parachute** (luh pa-ra-shut)   parachute
12. **la fusée** (la fu-zay)   rocket
13. **l'hélicoptère** (lay-lee-kop-ter)   helicopter
14. **le navire** (luh na-veer)   ship
15. **le bateau** (luh ba-to)   boat
16. **le sous-marin** (luh soo-ma-rIN)   submarine
17. **la péniche** (la pay-neesh)   barge
18. **le canoë** (luh ka-no-ay)   canoe

Questions

1. What should you have with you if you jump out of an airplane?
2. Name two vehicles that have two wheels.
3. Name a vehicle that travels under water.
4. What vehicle in this picture can go to the moon?

16. La ferme (la ferm)   The Farm

1. **le champ** (luh shON)   field
2. **le moulin à vent** (luh moo-lIN a vON)   windmill
3. **la colline** (la ko-leen)   hill
4. **la vallée** (la va-lay)   valley
5. **la chute d'eau** (la shut do)   waterfall
6. **l'église** (lay-gleez)   church
7. **le clocher** (luh klo-shay)   steeple
8. **la petite maison** (la puh-teet may-zON)   cottage
9. **la roue hydraulique** (la roo ee-dro-leek)   waterwheel
10. **le corral** (luh ko-ral)   corral
11. **l'écurie** (lay-ku-ree)   stable
12. **le tonneau** (luh to-no)   barrel
13. **le taureau** (luh to-ro)   bull
14. **le lasso** (luh la-so)   lasso
15. **le cow-boy** (luh ko-boy)   cowboy
16. **le cheval** (luh shuh-val)   horse
17. **le chapeau de cow-boy** (luh sha-po duh ko-boy)   cowboy hat
18. **la selle** (la sel)   saddle
19. **la vache** (la vash)   cow
20. **la fermière** (la fer-myer)   farmer
21. **le tabouret** (luh ta-boo-ray)   stool
22. **la traite** (la tret)   milking
23. **la houe** (la oo)   hoe
24. **le râteau** (luh ra-to)   rake
25. **la fourche** (la foorsh)   pitchfork
26. **la pelle** (la pel)   shovel
27. **le mouton** (luh moo-tON)   sheep
28. **le dindon** (luh dIN-dON)   turkey
29. **l'oie** (lwa)   goose
30. **la grange** (la grONj)   barn
31. **le foin** (luh fwIN)   hay

32. **le champ irrigué** (luh shON ee-ree-gay)   irrigated field
33. **l'épouvantail** (lay-poo-vON-tigh)   scarecrow
34. **le tracteur** (luh trak-tERr)   tractor
35. **l'ouvrier agricole** (loov-ryay a-gree-kol)   field hand
36. **le silo** (luh see-lo)   silo
37. **le grenier** (luh gruh-nyay)   loft
38. **la boue** (la boo)   mud
39. **le porc** (luh por)   hog
40. **la porcherie** (la por-shuh-ree)   pigpen
41. **la cage à poules** (la kaj a pool)   chicken coop
42. **la poule** (la pool)   hen
43. **le portail** (luh por-tigh)   gate
44. **la brouette** (la broo-et)   wheelbarrow
45. **l'atomiseur agricole** (la-to-mee-zERr a-gree-kol)   fruit sprayer
46. **le sac de blé** (luh sak duh blay)   bag of wheat
47. **la chèvre** (la shev-ruh)   goat
48. **l'herbe** (lerb)   grass
49. **le puits** (luh puee)   well
50. **la ferme** (la ferm)   farmhouse

Questions

1. Who is milking the cow?
2. Horses are kept in _____.
3. Name all the animals in the farm.
4. What do you call the place where hogs are kept?

17. Les animaux au zoo (layz a-nee-mo o zo) Animals in the Zoo

1. **la girafe** (la jee-raf) giraffe
2. **l'éléphant** (lay-lay-fON) elephant
3. **le zèbre** (luh zeb-ruh) zebra
4. **la marmotte** (la mar-mot) marmot
5. **le cerf** (luh ser) deer
6. **le lion** (luh lyON) lion
7. **le léopard** (luh lay-o-par) leopard

8. **le perroquet** (luh pe-ro-kay)   parrot
9. **le quetzal** (luh kayt-zal)   quetzal
10. **le rhinocéros** (luh ree-no-say-ros)   rhinoceros
11. **le koala** (luh ko-a-la)   koala bear
12. **le serpent** (luh ser-pON)   snake
13. **le chimpanzé** (luh sheem-pON-zay)   chimpanzee
14. **l'ours blanc** (loors blON)   polar bear

Questions

1. Name an animal with a very long neck.
2. Which animal lives in the Arctic?
3. Name two birds in this picture.
4. Which animal has antlers?

18. À la plage (a la plaj)   At the Beach

1. **les appartements** (layz a-par-tuh-mON)   apartments
2. **le phare** (luh far)   lighthouse
3. **l'île** (leel)   island
4. **la vedette** (la vuh-det)   speedboat
5. **l'embarcadère** (lON-bar-ka-der)   pier
6. **le surveillant de plage** (luh sur-vay-ON duh plaj)   lifeguard
7. **le cocotier** (luh ko-ko-tyay)   coconut tree
8. **le bord de la mer** (luh bor duh la mer)   seashore
9. **le nageur** (luh na-jERr)   swimmer
10. **la planche de surf** (la plONsh duh surf)   surfboard
11. **monter à cheval** (mON-tay a shuh-val)   horseback riding
12. **l'appareil-photo** (la-pa-ray-fo-to)   camera
13. **le bois flotté** (luh bwa flo-tay)   driftwood
14. **la radio** (la ra-dyo)   portable radio
15. **le sable** (luh sab-luh)   sand
16. **la chaise pliante** (la shez plee-ONt)   folding chair
17. **le parasol** (luh pa-ra-sol)   parasol
18. **le pique-nique** (luh peek-neek)   picnic
19. **le thermos** (luh ter-mos)   thermos
20. **la crème solaire** (la krem so-layr)   suntan lotion
21. **le ballon de plage** (luh ba-lON duh plaj)   beach ball
22. **l'empreint de pas** (lON-prIN duh pa)   footprint

23. **le coquillage** (luh ko-kee-yaj)   seashell
24. **les algues** (layz alg)   seaweed
25. **la palourde** (la pa-loord)   clam
26. **le château de sable** (luh sha-to duh sab-luh)   sand castle
27. **les palmes** (lay palm)   fins
28. **la bouée de sauvetage** (la bway duh sov-taj)   lifesaver
29. **les lunettes de plongée** (lay lu-net duh plON-jay)   goggles
30. **le palmier** (luh palm-yay)   palm tree
31. **la serviette de plage** (la ser-vyet duh plaj)   beach towel
32. **la rame** (la ram)   oar
33. **le canot à rames** (luh ka-no a ram)   rowboat
34. **la mouette** (la moo-et)   sea gull
35. **le phoque** (luh fok)   seal
36. **le radeau pneumatique** (luh ra-do pnER-ma-teek)   inflatable boat
37. **le lion marin** (luh lyON ma-rIN)   sea lion
38. **la vague** (la vag)   wave
39. **la hutte** (la ut)   hut
40. **le bateau à voile** (luh ba-to a vwal)   sailboat
41. **le ski nautique** (luh skee no-teek)   waterskiing
42. **le paquebot** (luh pak-bo)   ocean liner

Questions

1. What do you call an umbrella that protects you from the sun?
2. What are the children building?
3. Name the animals on the beach.
4. Where is "le phare" located?

19. Le cirque (luh seerk)   The Circus

1. **le poirier** (luh pwar-yay)   headstand
2. **les acrobates** (layz a-kro-bat)   acrobats
3. **le tigre** (luh teeg-ruh)   tiger
4. **le feu** (luh fER)   fire
5. **l'anneau de feu** (la-no duh fER)   ring of fire
6. **le fouet** (luh fway)   whip
7. **le dompteur** (luh dONp-tERr)   trainer
8. **le lion** (luh lyON)   lion
9. **la corde de sécurité** (la kord duh say-ku-ree-tay)   safety cord
10. **la ceinture de sécurité** (la sIN-tur duh say-ku-ree-tay)   safety belt
11. **le cavalier qui monte à cru** (luh ka-va-lyay kee mONt a kru)   bareback rider
12. **les plumes** (lay plum)   feathers
13. **le costume** (luh kos-tum)   costume
14. **la barbe à papa** (la barb a pa-pa)   cotton candy
15. **le clown** (luh kloon)   clown

16. **le public** (luh pub-leek)   audience
17. **le défilé** (luh day-fee-lay)   parade
18. **le monocycle** (luh mo-no-seek-luh)   unicycle
19. **la corde raide** (la kord red)   tightrope
20. **le filet de protection** (luh fee-lay duh pro-tek-syON)   safety net
21. **l'échelle de corde** (lay-shel duh kord)   rope ladder
22. **le maître des cérémonies** (luh met-ruh duh say-ray-mo-nee)
    master of ceremonies
23. **la perche** (la persh)   pole
24. **le trapèze** (luh tra-pez)   trapeze
25. **la trapéziste** (la tra-pay-zeest)   trapeze artist

Questions

1. Who is going through "l'anneau de feu"?
2. What is the boy in the audience eating?
3. What is the tightrope walker riding?
4. What object does the trainer have in his hand?

20. Les instruments musicaux (layz IN-stru-mON mu-zee-ko)
Musical Instruments

1. **la guitare** (la gee-tar)   guitar
2. **les maracas** (lay ma-ra-ka)   maracas
3. **la timbale** (la tIN-bal)   kettledrum
4. **les castagnettes** (lay kas-ta-nyet)   castanets
5. **la trompette** (la trON-pet)   trumpet
6. **le tambourin** (luh tON-boo-rIN)   tambourine

7. **le violon** (luh vyo-lON)   violin
8. **la basse** (la bas)   bass
9. **la mandoline** (la mON-do-leen)   mandolin
10. **le baryton** (luh ba-ree-tON)   baritone
11. **la harpe** (la arp)   harp
12. **le banjo** (luh bAN-jo)   banjo
13. **le saxophone** (luh sa-xo-fon)   saxophone
14. **la clarinette** (la kla-ree-net)   clarinet
15. **le piano** (luh pya-no)   piano
16. **le trombone** (luh trON-bon)   trombone

Questions

1. Name six instruments with strings.
2. Name five wind instruments.
3. What is "la timbale"?
4. Name an instrument that has a keyboard.

21. **Les mots d'action** (lay mo dak-syON)   Action Words

1. **se balancer** (suh ba-lON-say)   to swing
2. **écrire** (ay-kreer)   to write
3. **danser** (dON-say)   to dance
4. **manger** (mON-jay)   to eat
5. **rêver** (re-vay)   to dream
6. **dessiner** (day-see-nay)   to draw

écrire

7. **jouer** (joo-ay)   to play
8. **travailler** (tra-vigh-yay)   to work
9. **faire du patin à roulettes** (fayr du pa-tIN a roo-let)   to skate
10. **monter à bicyclette** (mON-tay a bee-see-klet)   to ride a bicycle
11. **s'étirer** (say-tee-ray)   to stretch

Questions

1. What do you do before playing a sport?
2. What do you do with a pencil?
3. What do you do with skates?
4. What is "danser"?

22. Les numéros (lay nu-may-ro)   Numbers

1. **un** (IN)   one
2. **deux** (dER)   two
3. **trois** (trwa)   three
4. **quatre** (kat-ruh)   four
5. **cinq** (sINk)   five
6. **six** (sees)   six
7. **sept** (set)   seven
8. **huit** (ueet)   eight
9. **neuf** (nERf)   nine
10. **dix** (dees)   ten

Questions

1. How many strawberries are there in the picture?
2. How many lemons are there in the picture?
3. How many flowers do you see in the picture?
4. How many peaches do you see?

23. Les formes (lay form)   Shapes

1. **le carré** (luh ka-ray)   square
2. **le losange** (luh lo-zANj)   rhombus
3. **l'étoile** (lay-twal)   star
4. **l'ovale** (lo-val)   oval
5. **le triangle** (luh tree-ANg-luh)   triangle
6. **le cercle** (luh ser-kluh)   circle
7. **le rectangle** (luh rek-tANg-luh)   rectangle
8. **le croissant** (luh krwa-sAN)   crescent

Questions

1. Name three shapes that have four sides.
2. Name one shape that has three sides.
3. Which shape looks like a star?
4. What is "le cercle"?

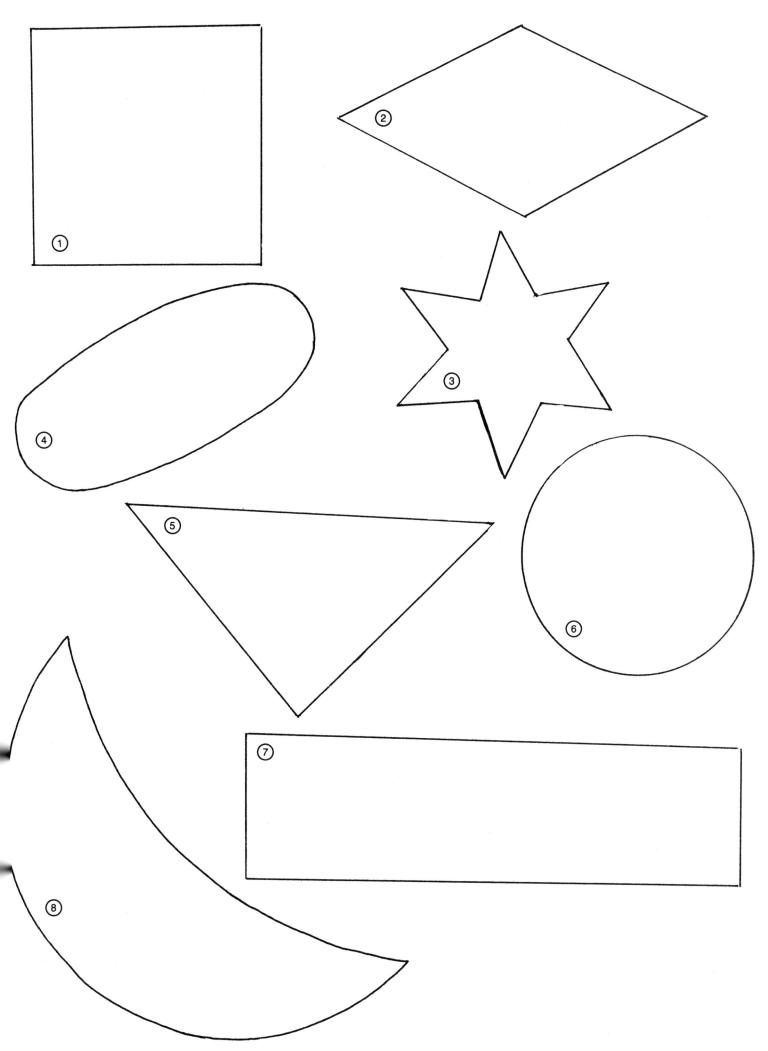

Réponses aux questions / Answers to the Questions

1. Notre maison

1. a watering hose
2. la pelle, la fourche à bêcher
3. la muraille en briques, la clôture en lattes
4. le jardinier

2. Le salon

1. les aiguilles à tricoter
2. le petit-fils
3. la pendule
4. le livre

3. La cuisine

1. le rôti de bœuf
2. l'eau
3. le pain grillé
4. le chiffon

4. En classe

1. les ciseaux
2. la soustraction, la multiplication, l'addition
3. la blouse
4. le dinosaure, l'horloge, la photo, le calendrier

5. Les vêtements

1. les lunettes
2. le pyjama
3. les chaussettes
4. le maillot de bain

6. Les saisons et le temps

1. l'arc-en-ciel
2. l'été
3. l'éclair, la pluie
4. la lune

7. Les sports

1. le base-ball
2. le ski, le ski nautique
3. le cyclisme
4. le bowling

8. La ville

1. l'accident
2. l'ambulance
3. le gendarme
4. a fireman

9. Au supermarché

1. la glace
2. les carottes, les choux, les choux-fleurs, les courges
3. la caissière
4. l'épicier

10. Au restaurant

1. le chef
2. la serveuse
3. le sandwich
4. le menu

11. La poste

1. la poste
2. l'adresse, le timbre
3. le facteur
4. a newspaper

12. La banque

1. le coffre
2. le coffre-fort
3. le garde
4. le bulletin de versement

13. Chez le médecin

1. le stéthoscope
2. le vétérinaire
3. l'infirmière
4. crutches

14. La station-service

1. le mécanicien
2. a bumper
3. la dépanneuse
4. le lave-auto

15. Le transport

1. le parachute
2. le vélo, la moto
3. le sous-marin
4. la fusée

16. La ferme

1. la fermière
2. l'écurie
3. le cheval, le taureau, la vache,
   le mouton, le dindon, l'oie,
   la poule, le porc, la chèvre
4. la porcherie

17. Les animaux au zoo

1. la girafe
2. l'ours blanc
3. le perroquet, le quetzal
4. le cerf

18. À la plage

1. le parasol
2. le château de sable
3. le cheval, le phoque, le lion marin,
   la mouette
4. l'île

19. Le cirque

1. le tigre
2. la barbe à papa
3. le monocycle
4. le fouet

20. Les instruments musicaux

1. la guitare, le banjo, la harpe,
   le violon, la basse, la mandoline
2. la trompette, le saxophone, le
   trombone, la clarinette, le baryton
3. a kettledrum
4. le piano

21. Les mots d'action

1. s'étirer
2. écrire
3. faire du patin à roulettes
4. to dance

22. Les numéros

1. deux
2. huit
3. trois
4. six

23. Les formes

1. le carré, le rectangle, le losange
2. le triangle
3. l'étoile
4. a circle